Success is not an Accident

This is a little book with a big Message

by

Dr Costakis Evangelou MBE

Copyright © 2015 Dr Costakis Evangelou MBE

ISBN: 978-1-326-48681-5

23/10/2019

with love

CW01497760

From HArchbishop

Evangelou

Disclaimer.

All information contained in this book is informative and given as a guideline, the reader must take full responsibility for any decisions he/she may take either in business or fitness, with health matters I encourage the reader before undertaking any fitness or dietary programs to consult with their Doctor, Optician, so that they can certify that there are no underlying medical conditions that would be detrimental to any diet or training programmes with regards to their physical wellbeing. The advice that I give is for information purposes only and it is the responsibility of the reader on how they use it. Having said the above, before making any decisions regarding your pursuit for success, make sure you are making an informed decision.

Dedication!

This book is dedicated to my family, friends and
all who strive for excellence!

A special thank you to Phodis C. Evangelou, Christopher
C. Evangelou, Julian Tobierre and Timothy Juuko for
proof reading the book, it is greatly appreciated!

Repetitio est mater studiorum
(Repetition is the mother of studies)

Contents

Forward by Julian Tobierre

Working as a sports coach brings a broad spectrum of people my way who come from diverse ethnic and cultural backgrounds. Many walk through the doors of the gym with an intention to achieve goals generally set by themselves. Sadly only the few seem to succeed in reaching their goals.

This begs the question is success an accident? In this short yet comprehensive book, Dr Evangelou takes the reader through personal and famous life examples, testimonials and quotes from the world of business to sport bringing to life the reality of what success truly is and how to achieve your goals.

One could not write such a book unless their own life achievements and experiences have led them to a conclusion. This book will offer the reader an opportunity to bring about a positive change in their lives by challenging them to think and step outside of the box.

About the Author:

A Profile of Dr. Costakis C. Evangelou MBE

Minister and Humanitarian

Currently holding the following qualifications, awards and positions of responsibility:

- Overseer of the Apostolic Christian Church (Sheepfold) in the Ecclesiastical Office of Archbishop.
- President of the Ixthus Church Council
- President of the registered charity, Community Heart (London)
- Honorary Secretary and Head Coach of the Edmonton Eagles Amateur Boxing Association
- Author of five books
- Completed two London Marathons successfully
- 2004 Made a Chief of Obomofodensua (Nana Oppong Gyan), Ghana, West Africa
- Dean of the Ixthus Church Council Bible College.
- Founder and Pioneer of the Eight Step New Testament Course, 'It's all Greek to Me'
- Professional Licenced Boxing Coach
- NLP Practitioner (Neuro Linguistic Programming)
- Qualified Full Boxing Coach
- Doctorate of Divinity
- PGCE in Religious Education
- BD (Hon) Theology

- 2008 - The Jack Petchey Foundation Leader Award Winner
- 2009 - Nominee for London Proactive Awards 'Coach of the Year'
- 2009 – Voluntary Youth Club Long Service Award
- 2009 – Obama Award for Outstanding Services to Society
- 2010 - Edmonton Local Hero Award, Inspiring Others
- 2014 – Invitation to Queen's Garden Party in recognition for outstanding work in the community
- 2015 – Received the Queen's Award for Voluntary Service (MBE for volunteer groups)
- 2019 – Received MBE in the Queen's New Years Honours List 2019 for services to Young People in North London

As well as the above; Dr Evangelou has produced two Music Gospel CD's; holds Music Qualifications with The Associated Royal Schools of Music and a Classical Performers Diploma with the London College of Music.

Introduction

I have set out to write a book that is small in content but big with regards to information, to help the reader look at life through different lenses.

We are living in a microwave generation we want everything here and now, in fact we want everything yesterday. Man's technology has become so advanced, we have every gadget under the Sun to save time yet, ironically we do not have enough time, our life is characterized by fast food, fast transport, yet we do not have time for the most important things in life, such as spending time with family, loved ones or a lifestyle that promotes our physical and spiritual wellbeing.

Often people spend so much time trying to make money and material wealth and when they have achieved this they spend all their wealth on doctors to try and regain the health they compromised while trying to become wealthy.

Through this book I would like to give the person who desires to be enriched and successful, various principles and keys to help him/her on their way to being successful.

Firstly I would like to define what I mean by success. Often people associate success with material wealth, i.e. a big house, a big car, a big bank account, these things are associated with success; in fact they are a by-product of success, but they are not the substance of success. Some people just want material things, but they do not give much thought or make any effort as to how they will obtain these things. In fact a successful person is a happy person, a successful person is someone who enjoys what he/she is doing, takes delight and pleasure with the things they are doing, and has a peaceful disposition. You cannot put a monetary price on a peaceful state of mind. Any monetary or material benefits are the by-products of this state of being.

This saying has been attributed to Marc Anthony:

"If you do what you love, you'll never work a day in your life".

People who are driven by the desire to make money must be careful not to affect their moral campus.

Maya Angelou has been quoted to have said:

"You can only become truly accomplished at something you love. Don't make money your goal. Instead pursue the things you love doing and then do them so well that people can't take their eyes off of you."

The dictionary definition of success according to *The Dictionay.com* is as follows:

Noun

1. the favorable or prosperous termination of attempts or endeavors; the accomplishment of one's goals.
2. the attainment of wealth, position, honors, or the like.
3. a performance or achievement that is marked by success, as by the attainment of honors:
The play was an instant success.
4. a person or thing that has had success, as measured by attainment of goals, wealth, etc.:
She was a great success on the talk show.

As we can see according to the dictionary definition success is not just about obtaining material wealth it is also about achieving goals, such as academic qualifications, a personal best in sport, or maybe losing weight. Yet for many people success is defined predominantly in terms of financial and material wealth. I would also like to encourage the reader to look at the concept of success in terms of a peaceful state of being.

Some people are driven by the desire to make money, so that it does not matter what they do, as long as they get money they are satisfied, this raises an ethical and moral question, does the end justify the means? Some people will compromise their integrity to satisfy their insatiable greed for money and material wealth. A point to make here is that this behaviour can have long-term negative emotional consequences.

Money may come and go but a peaceful disposition cannot be taken away.

History has shown that material achievements are not always secure as can be seen by these nine men who at their prime in life were the world's most successful financiers in the mid 20th century.

1. CHARLES SCHWAB was President of one of the largest steel companies.

2. SAMUEL INSULL was President of one of the largest electric utility companies.

3. HOWARD HOPSON was President of one of the largest electric & gas companies.

4. ARTHUR CUTTEN was the great wheat speculator.

5. RICHARD WHITNEY was President of the New York Stock Exchange.

6. ALBERT FALL was Secretary of Interior in President Harding's Cabinet.

7. LEON FRASER was President of the Bank of International Settlements.

8. JESSE LIVERMORE was the greatest 'Bear' on Wall Street.

9. IVAR KRUGER was head of the world's largest monopoly.

Yet according to my research I discovered that the end of their lives did not reflect their material achievements.

1. CHARLES SCHWAB lived on borrowed money for five years and died bankrupt.

2. SAMUEL INSULL died penniless in a foreign land.

3. HOWARD HOPSON turned [suffered with mental health related issues].

4. ARTHUR CUTTEN died insolvent.

5. RICHARD WHITNEY was just released from the Sing Sing Penitentiary.

6. ALBERT FALL was pardoned from prison due to ill health – nearly broke.

7. LEON FRASER committed suicide.

8. JESSE LIVERMORE committed suicide.

9. IVAR KRUGER committed suicide.

As I have been indicating money is the by-product of success, yet if you define success only in monetary terms you will be greatly disappointed.

I would like to look at one of the men in the list mentioned above, Jesse Livermore was known as the Bear of Wall Street. According to the information on *Wikipedia, the free encyclopedia*:

"During his lifetime, Livermore gained and lost several multi-million dollar fortunes. He sometimes played hunches, famously selling Union Pacific railroad short right before the 1906 San Francisco earthquake. Most notably, he was worth $3 million and $100 million after the 1907 and 1929 market crashes, respectively. Adjusted for inflation, $100 million in 1929, equals about in $1.384 billion in 2014, it would be over $125 billion today if put into Dow Jones Index with dividends reinvested. He subsequently lost both fortunes."

His story ends in tragedy as we continue to read:

"On November 28, 1940, Livermore shot and killed himself in the cloakroom of the Sherry Netherland Hotel in Manhattan. The police revealed that there was a suicide note of eight small handwritten pages in Livermore's personal notebook. It was reported in the November 30 issue of the *New York Tribune*. The press wanted to know what it said, and the police responded: "There was a leather-bound memo book found in Mr. Livermore's pocket. It was addressed to his wife." A police spokesman read from the notebook: "My dear Nina: Can't help it. Things have been bad with me. I am tired of fighting. Can't carry on any longer. This is the only way out. I am unworthy of your love. I am a failure. I am truly sorry, but this is the only way out for me. Love Laurie". From *Wikipedia, the free encyclopedia*

It is ironic that the man whom people looked to in terms of defining success, at the end saw himself as a failure. History has shown that when people are fixated on only power and material wealth they can lose themselves through the challenges and stresses of life. I would just like to add here that there is no problem having material wealth, but that should not be at the expense of compromising on a peaceful life. Do not spend time just trying to achieve material wealth, invest time in your peaceful disposition and enjoy the journey.

This leads me nicely to the question I would like to ask, "do you want to make money? Or do you want to be successful?"

Many people confuse the two, they think that making money equates to success, therefore we have to define what success is, there is the dictionary definition and there is the subjective definition of success, for many people accumulation of money equals success. I would like you to think for a moment with regards to this statement, "if a person is driven by making money, then does the end justify the means?" This book is not about how to become rich in the conventional sense of the meaning, I would like to suggest to the reader that monetary and material acquisition is a by-product of success and is not the substance of success.

Success is a lifestyle and is lived on an everyday basis. History has shown that people who are happy and enjoy what they do have longevity and are not affected by the objective circumstances that sometimes people encounter, because they do not base their lives solely on outcomes.

I am not for one moment suggesting that you do not plan for the future, or be like the ostrich and put one's head in the sand. What I mean is that a successful lifestyle is being able to adapt and use life's circumstances for the better and not let the circumstances and challenges in life dictate one's own happy disposition.

What is success?

Again we need to ask the question what is success?

I am not for one moment suggesting that one can live in an idealistic condition, we have to be realistic at the same time.

Therefore through this book I would like to help the reader finely tune his/her thought processes so as to be clear with regards to their desired goals and achievements, making their decisions from a rational informed position and not left to chance, as the title of this book says "success is not an accident". Before you embark on a journey you must first have your destination in mind, then you can take the necessary steps to get to the destination. When you get into a taxi you have to tell the driver where you want to go, no one enters a taxi and says to the driver, "just drive and I will let you know when I get there." This would be ridiculous, pointless and costly.

It is said, "Knowledge is power." I recall a story I was told a number of years ago regarding a wealthy ship owner. One of his big cruise ships engines had mechanical problems and would not start, so he called for an engineer to repair the ship's engine, when the engineer arrived he had in his hand a small tool bag, he looked around the engine a few times, took a hammer out of his bag, hit the engine in a particular place to which the engine began to work, the engineer left and said that he will send the owner the bill for the work.

The owner of the ship eventually received the bill it said, $100.000. The ship owner was taken back with the amount and instructed his secretary to ask the engineer to send him a breakdown of the invoice. The engineer sent back the break down that read as follows, $50.00 to hit the engine with the hammer, $99,950 for knowing where to hit the engine. The moral of the story is that knowledge is power. Therefore to be successful is not based on chance or luck, taking time and knowing the formula for achieving success in different fields in life will be beneficial to you.

For some people success is a hit or miss exercise, just imagine a sculptor throwing a piece of wood in the air and holding the chisel in his hand, hoping by chance that the wood would bounce enough times on the chisel to make an amazing piece of sculptured art. That sounds absurd and ridiculous, yet many people without realizing it live their lives by this principle.

Thought and preparation precede the actual sculpting of the piece of work, as there is a science to success. What I mean by science is that when certain principles are put in place success can be repeated in different fields.

Preparation is very important when regarding the outcome. There is an old maxim which says, "if you are not preparing to win, you are preparing to lose," this holds true with success, if you are not preparing to succeed you are preparing to fail. Some advice to bear in mind, enjoy the journey to your respective goals, dreams and visions, do this from a peaceful and happy disposition.

Note that happiness and peace should not be dependent on achieving your goals, because sometimes goals have to be changed for a number of reasons. Therefore if your happiness was dependent on a particular outcome and that outcome did not occur you could become a miserable person.

Adapting does not imply failure; it is just evaluating and modifying the process.

Sir Winston Churchill is quoted to have said:

"Success is the ability to go from one failure to another with no loss of enthusiasm."

We can substitute the word stepping stone or opportunity in place of failure.

We can also see the concept of failure as a process to success. It is a parenthesis on the road to success; it is a learning curve, it is not final unless one accepts it to be so.

Failure does not equal unhappiness and misery, you must be prepared to accept failure as part of the journey to success, the important thing is not to give up.

I have made some interesting observations in relation to how people respond when they are confronted with challenges or difficult situations in life. I have noticed that there are basically three types of attitudes people respond or react with; instinctive, emotional or rational.

Instinctive reaction:

Some people are driven by instinct, they react to a situation thoughtlessly, it is a survival mechanism. No real thought goes into instinctive action, for example the most basic level of instinctive reaction is that of a baby crying for food, this is the baby's survival mechanism, when the baby is hungry it cries out of a need for survival, therefore we can say instinct serves as an internal survival system that drives behaviour and it is not learned.

Emotional:

The second category of person is the one who reacts from the emotional level. Decisions are made from association with an emotion, traumatic or pleasant. There are different levels of emotions, but predominantly when an emotional person makes a decision it is based on an emotional experience they have had, good or bad. Emotional people are often caught up in the past emotions and never venturing forward out of fear, they discover that they repeat the same patterns, they feel as though they are going around in circles, and therefore making the same old mistakes, confirming the old maxim, "if you do what you did, you will get what you got."

Emotional reaction is a product of conditioning through different experiences in life.

Rational:

The third category of person is the rational person. They research and examine all the information and make an informed decision.

There is an attitude that is associated with success; to achieve one's desired goals and dreams you must have an optimistic attitude and the ability to adapt with regards to external situations.

Do not do things thoughtlessly; success begins in defining and knowing your goals. You have to discern your ability, and differentiate between imposed limitations and real limitations with regards to your vision and goals in your life; so that you begin with a clear understanding that the vision and goals you have are within your ability to achieve them.

For example if you are seventy years old and you want to run the Marathon, you have to ask yourself a number of questions. 1) Am I physically able to attempt this challenge? And 2) am I running for a personal best? Winning the marathon may not be a reality but finishing it is.

Therefore the success for this person is in finishing the race. Once this has been established every preparation surrounding the achievement must be put into place, i.e. times of training, diet, exercises etc.

This same principle is applied to any other area of achievement.

You must be prepared to take full ownership, control and responsibility for the decisions you make, so that you do not allow others to influence you and to determine your success or failure. It is important to receive the right advice from the correct qualified people; this will be beneficial in helping you to prepare and succeed. You must see the world through your eyes and not through other people's eyes; this will help you have the correct successful desired outcome in whichever area or field you choose to succeed in.

Characteristics of successful people:

Successful people have a vision. They believe in themselves.

Successful people have goals to aspire to, and no matter what people's opinions are about them, they persevere until they achieve their desired goals. For example look at Michael Jordan who was cut from his high school basketball team for "lack of skill"; he has now achieved legendary status in the sport.

Successful people have an inbuilt desire and tenacity that transcends every obstacle that life will throw at them.

Successful people use life's challenges as stepping-stones to reach their desired goals.

Successful people do not become victims of failure but become students and learn from life's experiences.

Successful people refuse to allow other people's limitations to encroach on their visions and goals.

Successful people take the "**t**" out of "can't" and say, "I can."

Successful people associate with likeminded people. Who you associate with has significant bearing with regards to achieving or not achieving your goals.

Environment and association also have significant bearing on a person's progress and journey to success.

I would encourage the reader with regards to cultivating a successful attitude to listen to inspirational music; read inspiring poems; watch inspirational and motivational films; listen to motivational speakers, all this will encourage a positive outlook in life.

Music is highly influential on a person's emotional disposition, as positive music lifts a person's spirit, and negative music can have a depressing effect.

When a composer wants to convey a happy bright sound with regards to a particular piece of music more than not he/she would employ the major scale, when a composer wants to convey a more solemn and melancholic sound they would employ a minor scale. These affect the recipient of the music. Music can create a sense of suspense, horror, tranquillity and much much more.

Association by music can be positive or negative depending on the state of mind the person is in when they hear a particular piece of music or song.

Also some people are affected by certain pieces of music that reminds them of their childhood, for example if the music was associated with fun and joy, then the emotions that were experienced are recreated. However if on the other hand, the experience was unpleasant and painful then listening to that particular piece of music would be unpleasant and can also be painful, depending on what that association reminds the person of will affect them either positively or negatively.

So, I encourage the reader to listen to music that is inspiring and brings back good memories and associations. If you are pursuing a fitness program then listen to music that will motivate you. The theme song to *Rocky Balboa* is one example of this. So explore and find the music and sound that motivates you.

From an ecological perspective we learn that different plants and different fruit grow in different environments and climates, you do not see palm trees in London, or fig trees in the North Pole. So depending on what you want to achieve you have to plant yourself in the correct environment to become productive. If you want to be an athlete you have to train in a sports environment, being in the Library all day would not serve this purpose.

Association, environment and attitude determine outcomes, whether they are positive or negative.

Your attitude in the correct environment has a great bearing on outcomes. For example, if you wanted to become a body builder just sitting in the gymnasium and looking at the weights and apparatus without participating will be of no benefit to you. It is engaging and participating that produces the results, in the same way you can be in a library looking at all the books, unless you engage and open the book and read, you will not increase your knowledge.

Association with the right people is very important, disassociation with wrong people is also very important.

In a garden we find many different types of plants, some wanted some not wanted, weeds grow with the other plants, the weeds are not wanted yet you find them in every garden, weeds are removed to help the other plants grow so that the garden is not overrun by the weeds, in the same way you need to choose your friends and not let them choose you, and be overrun with the wrong people, who, often or not, distract you from your desired goals. In fact the people who do not add to your life often take away your enthusiasm, dreams, goals and aspirations.

In nature we also discover that there are parasites that drain the life source of the host whom they make connection with, you must be careful that you are not drained by the wrong people who are around your life. To facilitate this way of life takes great resolve, character and sacrifice. Because when you do not dance to other people's tunes you run the risk of becoming very unpopular.

Remember whatever does not add to your life takes away from it!

The subject of disassociation is a very sensitive one, because many people are interconnected through emotional ties. Just because a person is geographically near you does not mean that they have your best intentions at heart. There is power in disassociation, it empowers you to propel and push you forward. You need to discern and differentiate with regards to people's attitudes around you. If you are in a negative, pessimistic environment where people are discouraging towards your dreams, visions and goals then you have to disassociate with these attitudes, otherwise you will become the product of that negativity.

There is proverb that says:

For as he thinks in his heart, so *is* he. (Pro 23:7 NKJ)

In the song by R Kelly called I believe I can fly, he says:

If I can see it, then I can be it
If I just believe it, there's nothing to it

[Chorus]

Hey, cause I believe in me, oh

If I can see it, then I can do it (I can do it)
If I just believe it, there's nothing to it

There is an amazing truth embodied within this song "I believe I can fly."

It is about vision, you need to see yourself in that place of success, once you can see it and believe you can achieve it, this attitude aids the outcome.

You need to see yourself in a particular position of success and believe that you can attain it, and then it is a matter of taking the necessary steps to achieve it.

Just as there is power in disassociation, there is power in the correct association; the people you connect with can either help open doors or close doors for you. Nothing can substitute good mentors, people you can look to for genuine guidance, people with experience who can help you to develop.

The Bridge

I would like to use a bridge as a metaphor to show the
wrong and right attitude to have when moving forward
to achieve your goals:

Drawing by my Granddaughter Kiara age 5

Some people will tread on people to cross over to
achieve their goals, I would just like to say that this has
long-term negative repercussions, one becomes
unscrupulous and not a pleasant and desirable person.

Other people thoughtlessly try to run and jump across without the need of a bridge; they leave it to chance as to whether they would reach the other side and achieve their goals, this can leave one bankrupt and emotionally shipwrecked.

The safer way is the calculated way; this is to lay a solid base and foundation.

Preparing and acquiring the wisdom from people who have already crossed over and who have already achieved their respective goals, this is a great benefit with regards to achieving your desired goals.

See your desired goals in terms of building a house. Look at the process involved when one has a vision to build a house. Everything begins with a thought; a vision of what is desired.

Then the thought is translated in terms of a 'blue print' with its dimensions, that is size of building, how many rooms, windows and so on. Costs involved are also taken into consideration, once everything has been agreed, the first part of the house to be prepared is the foundation. Now many try and put the roof first before any foundation and supporting walls, obviously there is nothing to hold the roof so they fail before they begin, this is a quick fix attitude, one must have something to hold the roof into place. Some people want the end but neglect the means to get to the end, for example you would think it is ridiculous to enrol for a three-year university degree and be awarded the degree without doing the coursework and sitting the examinations, or wanting to lose weight without dieting or exercise. Often it is the in-between part that people want to avoid, yet it is the in-between process that brings the outcome. Napoleon Hill is quoted to have said:

"Patience, persistence and perspiration make an unbeatable combination for success."

Coming back to our example for building a house, one also must take into consideration that depending on the height of the house this will determine the depth of the foundation, this is really something we call common sense, but to my surprise I have found that many people lack the capacity to see through the eyes of common sense. People often think in terms of outcomes and to their detriment they neglect the process.

Drawing by my Grandson Christian age 7

Therefore planning is very important.

If you are not planning to succeed, you are planning to fail.

Now set out the plan and sequence of steps for your respective goals.

Let's get started on your journey to success, remember success is also connected with knowing what you want to achieve in the first place, this is our starting place.

Make a list of goals you want to achieve.

Include timescales of when you want to achieve them.

The attitude you must have is one of enthusiasm.

Set the sequence of steps in quarterly timescales.

For example, if your goal is to lose weight set targets for yourself, put down how many pounds you want to lose per week. You need to have a journal to keep a daily record of your progress. You also need to have a diet plan that takes into consideration your calorie intake and an exercise routine. You must take into consideration your health and as I have mentioned earlier in this book, be informed with regards to any health matters that you need to consider, consult your Doctor and check if there are any underlying medical issues that you need to be aware of and get your Doctor's consent before embarking on any physical and dietary program. These are general guidelines; you have to take responsibility for your own wellbeing.

In life there is a general golden rule for success; "do not put off tomorrow the things you can do today."

If your goal is to return to university or start a company, start now. With the help of the Internet it makes life a lot easier to do your research.

If your dream and vision is to embark on a career in music, then become a student in the area you want to succeed in. If your desire is to play a musical instrument then firstly decide which instrument you want to play. As I have said earlier place yourself in the right environment, with the right people, that will help you understand the science of the particular instrument you want to master, and most importantly do not just look at the instrument, practice is of most importance.

In my younger days, I always had the desire to play the guitar, to be more precise I wanted to play the classical guitar, but because of financial restraints I could not afford a tutor, I was attending evening classes, but they were not adequate for me to progress on the level I wanted to. So I had to make a decision, do I just attend these classes and resign myself to the fact that concert level of performance was not for me or do I take an active response and do something about this situation, so I opted for the latter. I was so determined at the time to reach concert standard that I became my own teacher and learnt through every resource at hand, bearing in mind I did not have 'you tube', 'Google', or any of these resources.

I set myself a timetable for practise, I practiced five hours a day on the guitar until I knew every area inside out of the guitar, I could play with my eyes shut, and two hours a day I gave over to the theory of music. This was done five days a week. Within three years I qualified to grade eight in performance and grade eight in the theory of music with the Associate Schools of the Royal Schools of Music, and then I received the performers diploma (ALCM) with the London College of Music. From there I was teaching for the Inner London Education Authority (ILEA) in many of the Schools. Often I heard people say that they would love to play the guitar, or they would do anything to be able to play a musical instrument, my response to this was, "great!" PRACTICE! Having a good intention is one thing; making it a reality is something completely different.

I remember on one particular occasion in one of the classes that I was teaching, a young girl was attending who was blind. Within a few weeks I taught her to play the first part of the Spanish piece of music called *Romance*. For her it was a great achievement, she must have been 13 or 14 years old, this was in the early 1980's, her parents were so amazed that they wanted me to go to their home and give her private lessons. The reason that I am giving this testimonial is to show that with the right approach everything is possible, unfortunately some people make certain subjects very difficult to learn, they make them inaccessible. The philosophy that I go by is to take things that are perceived as difficult and simplify them. I would like to encourage the reader to explore and attempt to do things that perhaps he/she thinks are beyond their limitations, you may just surprise yourself.

I have applied this science of learning to many different subjects throughout my life, in sport, I have run a 5K Marathon and two London Marathons in two consecutive years, these were to raise funds for charities such as NSPCC and Great Ormond Street Children's Hospital as well many other charities. To run 26.2 Miles is not a walk in the park, preparation is of upmost importance, diet, training times, must all be calculated. You have to have a plan, I spoke with people who were runners about the nature of preparation, and I researched training programmes, I sourced the type of trainers I would need to be training with to lessen the impact on my knees and body. I ran with athletes, in the gyms on the treadmills, again I used the treadmills to lesson impact. The race was achieved in the preparation and training before the contest itself; repetition is the mother of perfection.

My advice to the reader is to get as much information as possible about the subject, career or business you want to do. Write down your goals on a paper and put them someplace where each day you can see them, to remind yourself not to give up.

Prepare a timetable that covers the week, keep to it, do not cut corners. As I mentioned earlier, enjoy what you want to do, and enjoy what you do, let it give you pleasure, do not decide to do something based solely on monetary benefits otherwise it will eventually become laborious and a chore, unpleasant and you will lose interest in it and not see it to its completion.

These principles can be applied in any field you desire to work in. Desire, determination, discipline, consistency and preparation, these are very important elements for success.

Do not become the victim of the limitations that people place upon you.

When I was a young child I vividly remember a day at Greek school where the teacher asked to see my father. He told my father not to waste money on sending me to learn Greek, because I could never learn to read and write the language. This gave me great pleasure because I did not like the subject, and, as a young boy of about 8 years old I would rather stay at home and watch TV or play in the streets with my friends. Yet later on in my life I have not only learnt the Greek Language but I have gone on to produce a course which is taught all over the world called *It's All Greek To Me,* not bad for a kid who was told that he would never learn the language!

Do not let others, even the so-called qualified people, determine or define your future. The thing is this, people do not understand the psychology of learning, you have to have the desire to learn, you must have the enthusiasm to want to learn, and of course you must enjoy the subject, you will only get great results if you really want to achieve a particular goal. Sir Winston Churchill said: "Never, never, never give up."

The battle is won or lost in preparation. I have three sons and one daughter, my eldest son Phodis is married with a beautiful daughter called Amelie, he is a qualified counsellor and at present he is studying for his Doctorate degree at Kings College, he has published a number of books, and is also in the sports field of boxing where we work together to support young boxers realise their potential. My two other sons Andreas and Christopher are professional boxers, both international champions, the older of the two is also the head of a mentoring unit in Enfield, London, the younger is now also pursuing a career in acting. My daughter Marisa is a personal trainer and also works in the beauty industry, she has two children Christian and Kiara.

Good preparation is nine tenths in my estimation of success, desire, determination, discipline, consistency and preparation are the keys that open the doors of success, for my sons to become international champions and achieve the honours which they have, has taken great discipline in their preparation, the question you also need to answer before you begin your quest to achieving your goals is how much do you want them?

There is no better time to begin than right now!

Before I conclude I would like to give a recent testimonial with regards to myself. On the 6th of June this year 2015, my son Christopher and I ran a seminar on the principles of success, I asked the people who attended to write their goals that they wanted to achieve and I then asked them to prioritize. So that they would look at primary goals. As the proverb attributed to Confucius says:

"a person who chases two rabbits catches neither."

Then we discussed in groups some of their goals and how they thought these could be achieved. We had excellent feedback, I used the pie chart as a basis to examine personal timescales; therefore depending on the areas they felt they wanted to develop and improve on with regards to their goals, they would adjust the percentages on their personal pie chart on a daily basis so as to maximize their potential for improvement.

Here is an example of a daily 24-hour pie chart:

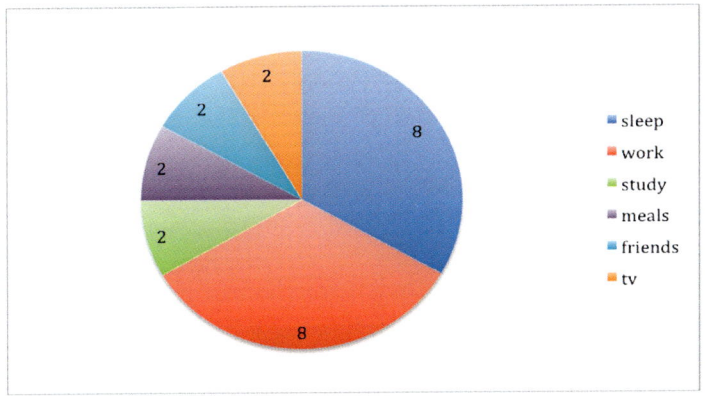

The above is a hypothetical pie chart, the numbers in the chart represent the hours per day, the colours on the right of the chart indicate the activity that is done throughout the 24-hour day. Now if this person wants to improve their health they will have to dedicate a portion of the day to a fitness program.

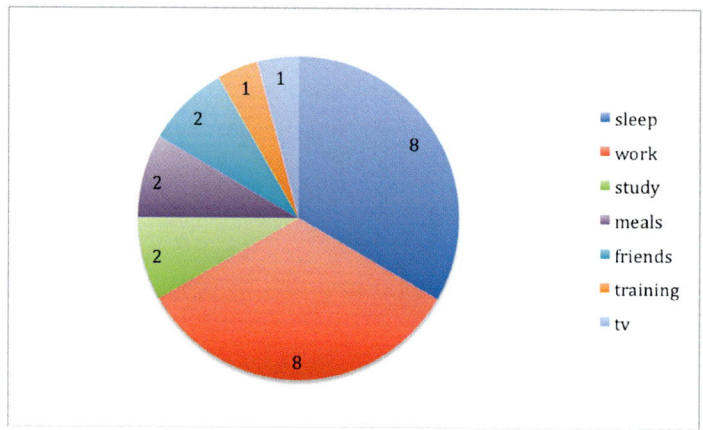

By adding an hour of program each day will impact on personal fitness and wellbeing, this will also have health benefits.

This is just one example, by adjusting the different segments on the pie chart will help improve the areas you want to develop in your life. For example, you may want to take a portion from sleep and dedicate this to study, reading or training. By adjusting the segments, this will have a positive effect in developing yourself in the area or areas you desire.

You may choose to spend less time with friends and less time watching TV and dedicate this time to developing your mind and fitness, in which case the pie chart will look like this:

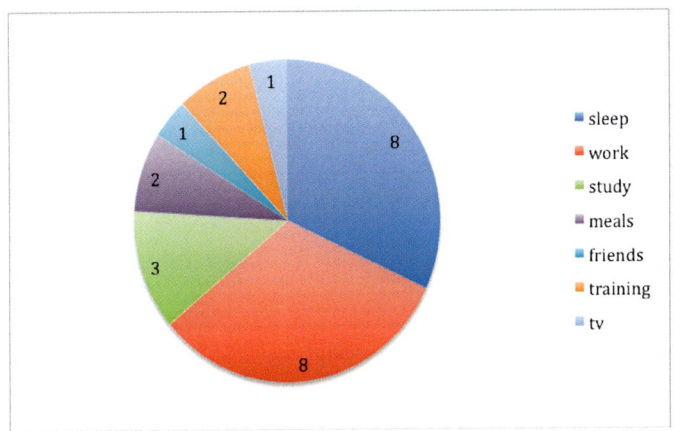

A note to the reader, by setting this chart in place do not stress yourself if you miss a session or for one reason or another you cannot keep to the chart 100 % all the time, but for best results try and keep to the schedule as best as you can.

The reason that I mentioned the principle of the pie chart is because this is the method I use when planning my desired goals. This year 2015 in April I was weighing 14 stones and 5 pounds, due to my travelling and neglecting a healthy diet I put on some significant weight, which also can have a negative impact on my health, therefore using the principles of the pie chart I included an hour of fitness for five to six days a week, I began writing this book in April 2015 at the time I was in Las Vegas with Christopher my son, my weight at the time was 14 Stones and 4 Pounds, we are now in September 2015 my weight is now 11 stones.

To give you an idea of the difference in approximately five months, I have included two photos below, before and after (the later photo was taken on the 19th September 2015):

Before April 2015   After 19th September 2015
14 stones 4 pounds   11 stones

Conclusion

It is pointless to write at length and just take up space in a book. The purpose of this little book is to motivate you, to inspire you, to encourage you, to help you believe in yourself and to put into practice the principles outlined in this little book, and see the positive outcomes. I am the eternal optimist, my cup is not just half full but over spilling and I want people to drink from my overflow.

I would like to conclude this little book with a few quotes from people who have inspired me through my life:

Jimmy Cliff: "You can get it if you really want it, but you must try."

Confucius says: "A man chasing two rabbits will lose them both."

Confucius says: "If you are hungry and stand with your mouth open do not expect a roast duck to fly into your mouth."

Sir Winston Churchill: "Choose a job you love, and you will never have to work a day in your life."

Steve Jobs: "First we need to define our understanding of the word success; people's perception differs with regard to their understanding of what it means to be successful."

The Apostle Paul: "I can do all things through Christ who strengthens me." (Phil. 4:13 New King James Bible Version)

And my final quote comes from Jesus who for me beautifully sums up everything:

"…all things *are* possible to him who believes." (Mk. 9:23 New King James Bible Version)

I wish you God speed and whatever your hand finds to do, do it with the best of your ability, that you become successful! May peace, joy, happiness be your portion! Enjoy the journey!

NOTES